The Forever Abode

Dustin Pickering

"Man—who crawls on all fours as a baby, then walks on two feet as an adult, and then uses a walking stick in old age."
-Oedipus

TRANSCENDENT ZERO PRESS

HOUSTON, TEXAS

ISBN-13: 978-1-946460-23-3

Printed in the United States of America

Transcendent Zero Press
16429 El Camino Real Apt. #7
Houston, TX 77062

Cover artwork: "Demeter Mourning for Persephone", Evelyn de Morgan, 1906
Cover Design: Glynn Monroe Irby

FIRST EDITION

The Forever Abode

Dustin Pickering

Fear and Trembling

Why my love do you draw the darkness from me?
Whose hand is being held in this tempestuous flight?
Two wings are not unknown to each other
and you are already aware of my smile.
O clever, the rain will lead us to sleep—
you holding my hand, and I bearing wounds.
So what of it?

Tell me who is in control of our flighty doom?
What penetrates our fears?
Having each other we have no need of fear and trembling.

I.Baby

wrack the gordian knot
of clouds
against grainy sky

because I honor you
because love isn't cheap—

my heart sequestered
by phantom desires

and touch what soul?

the days when last comes first
when darkness preens our bodies

flight like a whistle
birds of stone we cannot eat

I lay quietly in your light

but what's this I want enough
to live?
your flowery eyes!

shadows cast over my face
to darken winds of fear

golden silence floods your face
but I know how to climb
all energies

                by design I am fatal

horse of sleep carrying you
toward me
where dreams eviscerate the mind

and origin a bank of laughter
were we ever children,
        or two much between?

there, I see the flight of sparrows
foretelling your sleep
which wakes the door to perceive

and o such vast pleasure
in this field of flowing truth

you inhabit this tender world
with a majesty no one recognizes
        but me

your mirror hides your splendor
and it never gives it back

in the end we both stand on the bridge,
    clutching a dream, something starry by horrendous
fearsome and benevolent

looking into the still green waters—
where the angels grieved me.

you suggestively glance backwards
but I cannot see you

what bridge is this? did Hart Crane imagine
    flights of soul
on this tormented path?

o, but you walk…
finally I see,
there is nothing before me but smoke, fire, dandelions.
we left the bridge:
you walked north, I south,
and together we lost one another.

the efficacy of dawn
like hammers clutched to the skin—
tremulous magic
at earth's crust.

if rain falls, we will know our sense have awakened—
we fantasize on the eve of the morrow that gold is spawned
    by hurricanes—

love is a power, it steals at your waist.
and nothingness will reveal the shadows,
the shadows will raise the dead.

yes we satisfy, but no one knows the depths
of pain: the abyss of complete solitude.

sevendawn of deadly light—
quench me, make me real
because I don't know enough of this illusion.

a butterfly on the porch, sinking in flames
of power;
a butterfly on the veranda, teasing
your empathy.

if the hourglass is full at the bottom,
has beauty left the plaza sworn by fear?

how does she sleep in the staircase?
are wells of her eyes crying the foetus?
slumber like this dank dungeon of misery—
world, planet, spirit: all me.

look, leave: the trees are withering,
you are no longer among us
and I loved only you this whole time.

We Are Descending Together
After Marcel Duchamp's Nude Descending a Staircase, No. 2

I admit to my failure at lovemaking.
I don't make love; I destroy it.
It is in the hands of the spherical senses:
those balmy hands will keep it warm.
I am clueless—I can't hold you in motion.
Your private cinema is exposed
to my unenvied glances. I can't breathe.
Love in pursed plenty: dream,
the machine is voluminous and dark.
Heavy are the steel clutches that spring
to fear…empty energies part the Red Sea.

dispel myths and rumors
so tigers roam within the leaves—
orange and black, roses of plumage.

if peacock—some real lift from penury—
poor to the gallows lifted in sanctuary.

her hard back will crack a stone foundation,
colanders of madness.
crave sweet blackness.

in empty fear there is an impulse to love—
fear and trembling, not sweet showers of color:
only rainbows flee the waste of earth. and they return.

to you, my returning—
I look for your feet, I swallow the tinfoil
of my terror.
she bleeds like ink: nothing is there.

truth dictates like forgotten sorrow—
clutch, clutch, grim, grim.

if her light abides, longing fills the circle.
exit the tenth muse, nine will suffice.
what of god's adulterated passion?

I love with abandon—you will not forget.

bolt the doors, rinse your wings:
every fear is justified.
nightingale slit throat, stolen honey.

Sappho washes her feet.

yes, fathoms of forgetfulness
for I have forgotten you.
names are harbingers of detail,
speaking the plenary flights.

how do worms canker the flower?
envy's sweet bud purses its lips in song.

I glow surreal in the bedroom
like poems of foretold sweetness.

if one falls in love—what quaking
brings her back, stirring, like a dream?

she hangs her thought on gandered isles
while I pursue a thought of my own.
she is waking in startled breezes
coining her ApostropheSelf already old of guise.

did we make love like chaos waves make foam?
If I sing, will you even hear?

II. Adult

Poets know another Heaven,
a world of genuine sense,
full of knowing.

What is known is not what we are certain of,
but love soul's essence is primordial.
They held contests in the ancient world
to encapsulate your wit, charm, and beauty
long, long before light traveled to my eyes.

Like thirsting for wine from saintly reed,
her eyes crest the fallen magic
to attain a useless grandeur.
There is not a war in Paradise,
only fruits and cheese.

I unknot the collaborations of time,
stirring Fate's chalice,
pouring to the soil to stain the loved heart.

What I know I feel can never be pardoned.

Intuition and Destiny

Dark majesty, dark majesty,
an ancient ear to the flux,
her trust is intuitive.

What glory tells us
in the final grin
is reality is within.

Casual introvert,
brain saucy as the ways
of life:

kind face of brilliance,
each candle lit for favor,
her eyes are a temple.

Willing critic, unknown,
thoughts emerge and find justice.
Shadows ineluctable,

minor trembles of heart,
ancient pastime forgotten,
the poem is a rose—

eyes, gentle and serene,
soul spoken as a graft—
dear friend where heart bends.

in the light, in the ghostlight,
raw rooms of your honor,
thickened fear and fantasy.
there hangs an image of your illusion.

like a mirror squelched by fire,
ransom held like a baby,
your eyes meet a steady flippancy.
you do not know me.

I am not the wretched pile:
a body, stopped in slumber,
no fond memories of the day.
to gather the world in one whisper.

heaven is anonymous and there are raging flags
above us.
snapped in the wind, sought grievance.
are you failing the premise?
a movie never begins with a kiss.

your face illumines like moonglow—
o violent hazard of the faith,
such a straightened gate to the unknown.

weighted by the sun, morningtime
crucifies the earth:
an ancient song is buried.

your voice stills the starlit haze.
fog drifts through like a crippled clown.
camera focuses to your eyes, making serenity soft.
a glowering myth unnerved.

a child wakens in the bush.
his special ornament, fatigue of love.
he ages like a once cribbed orphan.

what does the god in the moment strive to impose?
we only see your hands, your ring of emerald.
like a sharpened wit, you level our assumptions.

hold the total powers:
nothing is senseless. Only the lack of sense.

laughter and mockery at the gate of thought:
I don't see the lamp's one thousandeth illumination.

perhaps it is an echo of something stolen in the dark.
rooms don't appear from schizophrenic swear words.
two-tongued reality slips its steady fork into the world.

however dream is assumed, real is deeper and further from our favor.

if a bold dancer of superb fancy catches the wind
in his teeth,
you will be born forever into my tired stanzas.

man as a gladiator:
woman as his mercy.

white stumps of senselessness:
a river escapes me.
but do you know where that river flows?

I am stone, blocking its fury mindlessly.

from my laden soul flows this timeless sea:
memories and longings unreserved in the deep.
a stark trek across middle earth.
only the destined arrive.

hunger tears into love's veins,
quaking in its soil,
blood dreaming its own tunnels of fire.
if there is a song in my head
it is one I wrote when I was dead.

the song masters our savagery.
total ambition with the old gray eyes.

clever war, inside the furrows of time:
all things built by pretense, shed pretense.
your eyes tell me the most amazing stories.

I enter your Paradise like Eve:
to steal a rose, to think of hope.
At birth I screamed shrill—
life is unbearable pardon, secrecy of depth.

but apple of my eye,
will you stand beside me in this graceful weather
where lunatics dwell, my mind their habit?

St. Francis stole a coat from his father
to help the poor. I am poor, my darling,
but I give my coat to you.
Now the world will not harm you.
I protect you with my careful eyes
because eyes eerily teach the heart to listen.

Thought burrows within souls of plenty,
burdened much by sweet sorrow.
We part, angels after the continuum.
Fire burns into your empty longing
as I ravage such delicate features
with my sharp wit.

you are not imbecile,
not fear. you are my glory,
and for you I bring the most caring
of creatures:
the moth.

if it does not recognize the flame—
it will burn of its own languished thought.
                    solitude grants me an open ear.

to be silent is a whore's promise—
sickness, the feeling of death over one's mouth.
if thoughtless con-artists know your name
you are wiser than the streets you parade.

fickle and bittersweet, horse of yellow
with stark gazing eyes:
I don't feel the surge of limitlessness.

Freud's oceanic feeling is dust in my mouth.
what the pathetic know only I cherish
with rings around my golden heart:
you, tide's keeping, master of cycles.

I seek you in snake chariots, fire blazing in my eyes,
head of stone, washed per senses meek,
the mirror gazed back to Jason.

An Argonaut futilely engaged in stripping the closets bare.

mystic fire of the path:
leaves fallen from branches
seeking the final hum of life.

as courtesy makes you a mirror dancer.
I can only love once, truly, and my energies
are exhausted.

burnt cauldron: thoughtless flights of domain.
a curve in space-time curse.
watchful engines bathing beside your tidal crossing.

o sight, develop an optimism of death:
final focus on one's soft room where the crows wait.
if a murder, then nothing will sing
the gallantry of time.
time, kisses wet, has recalled the music

and the dancers are slowly making way
for the reality of reunion.

III. Walking Stick

*For he lives with the least worry who knows not his misfortune;
but for humans, the best for them is not to be born at all, not to
partake of nature's excellence; not to be is best, for both sexes.
This should be our choice, if choice we have; and the next to
this is, when we are born, to die as soon as we can.*
-Silenus

sex and death are on the rainbow's path,
cold arms flying, thick sweat following the cast.
gentle, expectant, a noose of light surrounding your birth.
if I was perfect your stars would engage me.

such clutter of the mind, mound of empty sighs,
god is not with us: instead, within.
I grieve in your wake as solemn marchers pass—
tensions of bl
iss and strife,
waging the horror alone.

silence of need, stalk of wet tears still conveyed
to the flesh,
wed to a lost speech:
details to my heart.

I sign the march of triumph:
you are such as the rose will wake.
before you, there were complete silences.
smashed as a dreamer by the sliding rocks,
fault line casting chaos to our nouns.

you read my gaze like a flowered bee,
a comfort, golden, furtive and final.
we aren't looking for old age.

first lines are the most unusual—
this, however, is not the first line.
It is the final casting call.
Curtains down, shadows immersed in flame,
the devil must have entered from the annex.

behind the sun there is haunting.
atoms split, spill, and devour all mercies.

resist the proximate.
think harder on the selfless face
of God, who Almighty will render the talk useless.
inspiration or aspiration,
her bones are love's deeper wish.

when I cast my nets,
she will slip ashore like a causality—
bitter salt and seaweed deepened in the darkness.
thoughts parallel to this jive,
searching the mind for its last tones.

last rites of wickedness.
a touch of poverty, above the line—
water lines with the magic trust of sea.

doubt's deluge fosters forbidden senses.
if a monster I am, let me galvanize the pretty flux of death.
rapid sleep, dream in agency, I will not forgive.
the dirt is otherwise fertile.

hold my past accountable for its density.
heavy dream, laden with danger and heat.
curb the excess with idea and immensity.

livid as the sun after falling,
the trees turn to stone,
thoughtlessly a chamber of silence.
boundaries curve the fragile past;
touch it with water and violence.

don't let the enemies of former lovers
exclaim your plight to the world.

covet the rain but it let it fill your heart with love.

come with me, be a friend, think with me
such priceless thoughts:
the shell of your being is my hiding zone.
teach me what I can get away with.

if prayer and fortune are no better than chance,
sublime randomness rules the punch—
we dig in, we live, the banquet of folly
encounters us by chance.

slipping in the grief of time, weaving the circus
with the sword:

and wait, the quake will mesmerize such caution.

why does beauty insist on transgression?
do your eyes catch the latch and devote to power?
how subliminal—this simple exit wound.
you tie me to the irony of satisfaction.

why does beauty die on the fields?
wars depopulate, virgins deflowered.
the depths spring from my heart to caress the abyss—
there, only one bright soul at the hill.

storms tear at the edge of the cloth,
one hour at a time,
one hour at a time,
and the sun fills the temples with gold.
gold that is not purchased, but forgiven.

winter reaches me in slumber
and I die of a hurt once received.
I will not forget my love, for she is silver
to gestalt eyes.

the coldest strain of an unheard melody
stitches the wounds while blinding her fears.
to touch is one ruthless scenario.

I cannot believe your trust
or its electric dance. music is not clumsy.
between each planet, humming persists
as our eyes glaze each other like a lucid dream.
reality is not the question if there is an answer.

I want to trust your intention but you are not ready.
I know the crossing here; your wisdom strains the dross
of hearts in petty sloth.
Call out your own wrath and spill it in the wells.
Poison your own violence. Think straight thoughts.

Gold chalices are floating in an array of fleecy torpor:
wind puts the candle to its test. Failure is only a game.

It doesn't matter how or when—
love will sink into you like a raw fruit
seeded by memory.
The thought of you reconciles me to death.
Pulp and power are needy lies.

Step carefully at this golden threshold!
You will not see me again.
We have lived our worlds into their own dust,
cramping magic into a twisted hole.
Do not make this public.
It is a dying ritual only you and I share.

desert mountains guard the wind.
old wicker cabinets seize your curiosity
to trust my hands and feet.
what I do not kiss in gallantry
I will save for the driest heat.
plum radiation from the sky
bruises the surface of your kindness.
legs outstretched, hope embezzled from immolation,
I see the seriousness behind you.
Shadow of desperation:
will I call the bluff?

High priestess of winter's lodge,
thought's servant in espionage,
kyrie kyrie if only phantom suicides
will keep their watch over me.

speak of the elegy, to flow the river time
from my stained aperture:
such that the faery nicks the tree with her boots,
carrying her promise to another in dire flight.

www.ingramcontent.com/pod-product-compliance
Lightning Source LLC
Chambersburg PA
CBHW051050030426
42339CB00006B/290